Adorable
dogs

EDITED BY
HELEN EXLEY

BARNES
& NOBLE

NEW YORK

Whoever else thinks

you are of little worth—

to your dog you are

the heart

of his universe.

PAM BROWN

A quiet, gentle dog
will bring a quiet,
deep satisfaction
to your whole life.

HELEN EXLEY

quiet and gentle

joy of living

W hatever is, is good—your gracious
creed. You wear your joy of living like a crown.

DOROTHY PARKER

He is born our friend;
while his eyes are still closed,
already he believes in us:
even before his birth,
he has given himself
to man.

COUNT MAURICE
MAETERLINCK

The average dog has one request
to all humankind: love me.

HELEN EXLEY

A man's best friend

is his dog. LORD BYRON

To your dog, you are

more than just a friend;

you are the leader of the pack,

his protector, his provider,

and an all-knowing god.

STUART & LINDA MACFARLANE

...once a dog

...once a dog loves you,
it loves you always,
no matter what you do,
no matter what happens,
no matter how much
time goes by.

JEFFREY MASSON

loves you

Happiness is a warm

puppy

CHARLES M. SCHULZ

my little

My little old dog:
a heartbeat
at my feet.

EDITH WHARTON

dog

Dogs bring out the best in humankind.

PAMELA DUGDALE

the only love

Puppies for sale:
The only love
that money can buy.

SIGN ON BULLETIN BOARD

money can buy

...I felt a silent current of love
from him—strong, steady and deep...
For someone who has never
had this kind of experience...
there are no words to adequately
explain it.

SUSAN RACE

Rarely did he take his beautiful,
kind eyes off me…
and wherever I went there he would be too,
and wherever I sat he would…
sit beside me, close, protecting me,
his head on my knee.

ELIZABETH VON ARNIM,
FROM *ALL THE DOGS OF MY LIFE*

l o v e l i n e s s

To hold a living creature, to learn its loveliness,
to feel its heart beat in our hands,
to know its trust, is at last to understand
that we are kin. Is to rejoice in life.
Is to lose all loneliness.

PAM BROWN

Dogs, no matter
their breed, all have
an inner beauty.
They have
kind, gentle hearts
and a real need
for company
and affection.

STUART & LINDA MACFARLANE

happy

People need a measure
of happy simplicity—
and a dog supplies it.
Unqualified love,
and very
few demands.

CHARLOTTE GRAY

simplicity

c o

A life, a warmth,
an intelligence.
A kind companion.
A dog.

PAM BROWN

mpanion

How can any of us
explain how we feel
at that first moment,
in the early morning,
when the animal we have chosen
to share our lives is waiting
for the pleasure of our presence.

JOYCE STRANGER

Soft big eyes,
gentle and quiet.
She is patient and loving
—just what any
stressed-out
human needs.

HELEN EXLEY

believes

n you

A dog believes
you are what you
think you are.

JANE SWAN

He will kiss the hand that has no food to offer.... He guards the sleep of his pauper master as if he were a prince.

SENATOR GEORGE VEST

so sad

Every dog deserves

a smile, a word of admiration,

a little reassurance

—especially if he is very ugly

or very sad.

PAM BROWN

fuzzy fur

Dogs are
effervescent,
fuzzy marvels
of nature.

MARI GAYATRI STEIN

Dogs come in
all shapes and sizes,
Yet every one,
you must agree,
Make humans
perfect company.

STUART & LINDA MACFARLANE

perfect company

Dog, *n.*

A kind of additional

or subsidiary Deity designed

to catch the overflow

and surplus of the world's worship.

AMBROSE BIERCE, FROM *THE DEVIL'S DICTIONARY*

Heaven goes by favor. If it went by merit,
you would stay out and your dog would go in!

MARK TWAIN

A dog knows that if he sits in front of you long enough and pleads with every look and wag, you'll eventually give in and take him for a walk.

PAM BROWN

pleading

Puppies look like very small children whose mothers have bought a size or two too big clothes. To give them growing room.

MAYA V. PATEL

floppy

puppies

…adorable little puppy
who will snuggle up
to you, nibble your ear,
gambol and romp
all over the place…
worming its way
into your heart,
making a slave of you….

BUSTER LLOYD-JONES

What can we call them;
A huddle of pups?
A wriggle of pups?
A squirm, a shove
A muddle of pups?
A drowse of pups.
A sprawl of pups.
A totally out of this world of pups.
And all gathering the energy
to become a rush, a plunge,
a stampede of pups.

CLARA ORTEGA

They have a new puppy next door. I heard him singing in the night—a most mournful song of loss—mother and siblings, remembered smells and familiar faces.

No matter that his new bed is soft, that the light has been left on, that food and water is within reach. It is all too strange, too large, too lonely. He tries his range of voices—pleading, whimpering, howling—but no one comes. He is lost forever in a huge and unfeeling universe.

A week later and I meet him. The house is his. Bed, blanket, food dish, people. He greets me as a friend. All the world loves him—he is content.

CHARLOTTE GRAY

Your little dog
has never even seen a rabbit—
but watch when he's asleep.
He's chasing down
a mammoth.

PAM BROWN

little hunter

The smart dog quickly discovers that, to get what he wants, one mournful look is much more effective than a frenzy of barking.

STUART & LINDA MACFARLANE

All right, so I don't know how to bury my garden messes. And I bark at everything. And I'm not very good at washing myself. And I roll in doubtful substances. And I smell a bit iffy in warm weather.

But I love you, love you, love you, and I will go on loving you till the day I die…

PAM BROWN

What jolly chaps they are!

They are much superior

to human beings as companions.

They do not quarrel or argue with you.

They never talk about themselves,

but listen to you

while you talk about yourself.

JEROME K. JEROME, FROM *IDLE THOUGHTS OF AN IDLE FELLOW*

A dog likes to sit
under the dining table.
Just in case.

PAM BROWN

We believe in ourselves because of the trust our puppy has in us.

MARGOT THOMSON

He is your friend, your partner, your defender, your dog. You are his life, his love, his leader. He will be yours, faithful and true, to the last beat of his heart.

AUTHOR UNKNOWN

A wise dog
can teach us much
of what we need to know:
Patience.

Caring.

Companionship.

And Love.

PAM BROWN

Most of us suffer from too much tension and stress in the hustle of modern urban living, where minute-by-minute considerations are frequently complex and demand a whole range of conflicting compromises. By contrast, the friendly contact of a pet dog or cat serves to remind us of the survival of simple, direct innocence even inside the dizzy whirlpool we refer to as civilization.

DESMOND MORRIS, FROM *DOGWATCHING*

How strange to think Dog was once simply Dog.
For see how we have squashed him and stretched him.
Yet inside every variation
is that first and utterly basic Dog.

PAMELA DUGDALE

E<small>VERY</small> dog
is beautiful
in its own way.

STUART & LINDA MACFARLANE

U S T

A dog will continue to trust when it has been betrayed.

So my good old pal,
my irregular dog,
my flea-bitten,
stub-tailed friend,
Has become a part
of my very heart,
to be cherished till
life-time's end.

W. DAYTON WEDGEFARTH, FROM "BUM"

Here's love.

Disguised as a mop.

PETER GRAY

Montmorency's ambition in life
is to get in the way and be sworn at.
If he can squirm in anywhere
where he particularly is not wanted…
he feels his day has not been wasted.

JEROME K. JEROME,
FROM *THREE MEN IN A BOAT*

BONES
BONES
BONES

If a dog's prayers were answered,
bones would fall from the sky.

PROVERB

He toils not, neither does he spin, yet Solomon in all his glory never lay upon a door-mat all day long, sun-soaked and fly-fed and fat, while his master worked…to purchase an idle wag of the Solomonic tail, seasoned with a look of tolerant recognition.

AMBROSE BIERCE, FROM *THE DEVIL'S DICTIONARY*

the silent

stare

…if he wanted a dog biscuit, he simply sat near the box
of biscuits and silently stared at one or the other of us.
If he not merely wanted a biscuit but felt
it was positively his right to have one, the silent
stare was accompanied by a lowering
of the head…

GEORGE PITCHER, FROM *THE DOGS WHO CAME TO STAY*

Even asleep, he will detect someone

scraping out the last remnants

of Marmite from the jar in the kitchen

four floors below

and thunder downstairs to lick it clean.

TREVOR GROVE

${\rm D}$og's maxim

on relaxation:

The secret to being

completely relaxed is

to have a human to do

all the worrying for you.

STUART & LINDA MACFARLANE

One rattle of the biscuit tin
and you've got friends for life.
They sit and stare
with solemn eyes,
and if you don't take the hint,
you get barked at.

JANINE CHUBB

A dog's only
ambition is
to give you
all his love.

STUART & LINDA MACFARLANE

The world
would be a sadder place
without puppies.

PAM BROWN

puppies

Just a scruffy little dog…
And yet you are the best,
the kindest friend
anyone could have.

MARGOT THOMSON

At times it was like gazing into a human soul,
to look into his eyes; and what I saw there frightened me.
I tell you I sensed something big in that brute's eyes;
there was a message there, but I wasn't big enough myself
to catch it…it gave me a feeling of kinship all the same.
Oh, no, not sentimental kinship. It was, rather,
a kinship of equality.

JACK LONDON, FROM *THAT SPOT*

KINSHI

P

Happy is the dog

who has found a kind human

—he will forever have

someone to tickle his tummy.

STUART & LINDA MACFARLANE

'Tis sweet to hear
the watch-dog's honest bark
Bay deep-mouth'd welcome
as we draw near home;
'Tis sweet to know
there is an eye will mark
Our coming,
and look brighter
when we come.

LORD BYRON, FROM "DON JUAN"

Poor dog! He was faithful and kind to be sure,
And he constantly loved me although I was poor;
When the sour-looking folk sent me heartless away,
I had always a friend in my poor dog Tray.

THOMAS CAMPBELL, FROM "POOR DOG TRAY"

Your dog just doesn't notice that you are old or ill or unsuccessful.

To him you are perfect.

PAM BROWN

While I run my toes over his arched spine, I actually feel my tension easing and my bunched up muscles relaxing. I imagine (as most dog owners invariably do) that he "understands" me, understands what I'm saying to him.

SHOBHA DÉ, FROM *SPEEDPOST*

relaxing

...we simply loved them
with all our hearts;
we perhaps even loved them—
I'm not ashamed to say—
beyond all reason.
And they loved us, too, completely,
no holds barred.
Such love is perhaps the best thing
life has to offer.

GEORGE PITCHER, FROM
THE DOGS WHO CAME TO STAY

I have found

that when you are deeply troubled

there are things you get

from the silent devoted companionship

of a dog

that you can get

from no other source.

DORIS DAY

Keesha was my friend, my confidant, my angel and, ultimately, my teacher.

SUSAN CHERNAK MCELROY

confidant,
angel, teacher

The rich man's guardian
and the poor man's friend,
The only creature
faithful
to the end.

1

your

He is going to stick to you,

to comfort you,

guard you, and give his life

for you, if need be…

You are his pal.

JEROME K. JEROME, FROM *IDLE THOUGHTS OF AN IDLE FELLOW*

pal

THE *ADORABLE DOGS* TEAM

Yoneo Morita, who took the stunning photographs in the book, was born in Ito, Japan, in 1950. He graduated in photography in Tokyo, and after working in a photographic library, has spent more than a decade capturing thousands of people's pets on camera. He adores dogs (he and his wife have twenty cats and six dogs in their own home), and has the patience—sometimes taking a week or more—to gain the friendship and acceptance of all his "models." This enables him to get the humorous, trusting, and intimate "fish-eye" shots that have become his trademark. Yoneo Morita's work, with its familiar Hanadeka ("big nose") emblem, is now licensed to publishers and manufacturers in more than twenty countries around the world.

Helen Exley has edited and published several hundred books using her unique collection of quotations. Her books have appeared in more than fifty languages and are exported to over seventy-five countries. Helen Exley personally chose all the quotations to match Yoneo Morita's photographs in this volume, and hugely admires his work. "I work with writers, illustrators, and photographers across the world, and I regard Yoneo Morita as the top dog photographer of his time. He is a master of his art, and the results are just enchanting."

PERMISSIONS